The ice was melting fast in the Arctic Ocean.
Koa watched the ice melt with his parents,
Mama Polar Bear and Papa Grizzly Bear.

Monterey Coates

The Kind Bear

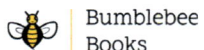
Bumblebee Books

BUMBLEBEE PAPERBACK EDITION

Copyright © Monterey Coates 2025

The right of Monterey Coates to be identified as author of
this work has been asserted in accordance with sections 77 and 78 of the
Copyright, Designs and Patents Act 1988.

All Rights Reserved

No reproduction, copy or transmission of this publication
may be made without written permission.
No paragraph of this publication may be reproduced,
copied or transmitted save with the written permission of the publisher, or in
accordance with the provisions
of the Copyright Act 1956 (as amended).

Any person who commits any unauthorised act in relation to
this publication may be liable to criminal
prosecution and civil claims for damage.

A CIP catalogue record for this title is
available from the British Library.

ISBN: 978-1-83934-971-3

Bumblebee Books is an imprint of
Olympia Publishers.

First Published in 2025

Olympia Publishers
Tallis House
2 Tallis Street
London
EC4Y 0AB

Printed in Great Britain

"The ice is melting faster every year,"
said Mama Polar Bear sadly.
She depended on the ice to survive.
"Yes, the ice is melting faster and faster every year,"
agreed Papa Grizzly Bear.

The fast-melting ice was the reason
Mama Polar Bear met Papa Grizzly Bear.
The fast-melting ice meant that
the climate was getting warmer
in the North where usually only polar bears,
like Mama Polar Bear, lived.

The warmer climate in the North meant
that some grizzly bears,
like Papa Grizzly Bear, travelled from the land
in the South to the fast-melting ice in the North.

Papa Grizzly Bear had travelled a long distance from the land in the South to the fast-melting ice in the North to meet Mama Polar Bear. Mama Polar Bear and Papa Grizzly Bear had fallen in love and had Koa, an unusual polar-grizzly bear mix.

Soon Koa would be old enough to leave
Mama Polar Bear and Papa Grizzly Bear.
Koa was worried because he did not know where
he was going to live or who
he was going to be when he left
Mama Polar Bear and Papa Grizzly Bear.

Koa was not a normal polar bear so he did not want to live only on the ice.
Koa was also worried about how fast the ice was melting each year in the North.

Koa was not a normal grizzly bear so he did not want to live only on the land.
Koa was also worried about travelling all the way to the land in the South.

"Where am I going to live when I leave?"
Koa asked Mama Polar Bear.
"Who am I going to be when I am older?"
Koa asked Papa Grizzly Bear.
Mama Polar Bear and Papa Grizzly Bear
both looked at Koa.

Just as Mama Polar Bear and Papa Grizzly Bear were about to answer Koa, there was a very loud noise.

CRAAAACKKKK!

Mama Polar Bear, Papa Grizzly Bear,
and Koa looked to see
where the loud noise was coming from.
Humans! Humans were on a boat using machines to
crack open the fast-melting ice.

"Run!" yelled Mama Polar Bear.
"Fast!" shouted Papa Grizzly Bear.
Koa started to run away from the cracking ice and loud human noises. Koa ran faster and faster.

Koa kept running until he could not hear the loud human noises.

Then Koa looked around. Where was Mama Polar Bear? Where was Papa Grizzly Bear?

Koa walked back towards the loud human noises to look for Mama Polar Bear and Papa Grizzly Bear.

Just as Koa was getting close
to the loud human noises, he heard
another very loud noise from behind him.

GRRRRRRRRRR!

A grizzly bear! A grizzly bear growled at Koa.
"I am lost!" said the lost grizzly bear to Koa,
"I am from the land in the South.
The forest that I lived in caught on fire and I need to find
a new forest to live in! I need to find my way
to another forest in the South!"

"I can help you," said Koa to the lost grizzly bear.
Koa was very good with directions and knew which way
was North and which way was South.
"This is the way to the land in the South,"
Koa pointed, "I can walk with you."

Koa walked with the lost grizzly bear
until the lost grizzly bear
could see the forest in the South.
"Thank you," said the lost grizzly bear to Koa,
"you are a very kind bear."

Koa said good-bye to the lost grizzly bear
and walked North towards
the loud human noises to look for
Mama Polar Bear and Papa Grizzly Bear.

Koa found some berries to eat along the way.
Koa took some extra berries for later.

Just as Koa was getting close to the
loud human noises, he heard
another very loud noise from behind him.

GRRRRRRRRR!

A polar bear! A polar bear growled at Koa.
"I am so hungry!" said the hungry polar bear to Koa,
"I am from the fast-melting ice in the North.
The ice that I lived on melted and I cannot find food to eat!
I need to find my way to more ice in the North!"

"I can help you," said Koa to the hungry polar bear.
Koa gave the hungry polar bear his
extra berries and told him
where to find more ice in the North.

"This is the way to more ice in the North," Koa pointed, "I can walk with you."

Koa walked with the hungry polar bear
until the hungry polar
bear could see more ice in the North.
"Thank you," said the hungry polar bear to Koa,
"you are a very kind bear."

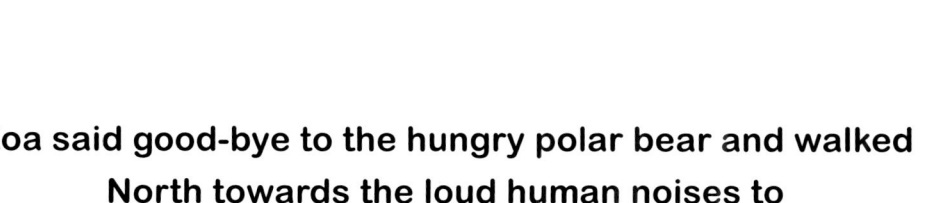

Koa said good-bye to the hungry polar bear and walked
North towards the loud human noises to
look for Mama Polar Bear and Papa Grizzly Bear.

Just as Koa was getting close to the loud human noises, he heard another very loud noise from behind him.

GRRRRRRRRR!

Mama Polar Bear! Papa Grizzly Bear!
Mama Polar Bear and Papa Grizzly Bear stopped
growling when they saw Koa.
"We thought you were a human!"
cried Mama Polar Bear.
"We are so glad that we found you!"
cried Papa Grizzly Bear.
"Me too!" cried Koa.

Koa looked happily at
Mama Polar Bear and Papa Grizzly Bear.
"You know," Koa said, "I still don't know where
I am going to live or who I want to be when I am older…"

"...But I do know that no matter what I want to be a kind bear," smiled Koa.

"That's the best type of bear," smiled Mama Polar Bear.
"The very best!" smiled Papa Grizzly Bear.

About the Author

Monterey Coates grew up near the Canadian Rocky Mountains with her parents and older brother. She has a Bachelor of Science in Geology and a Bachelor of Education. *The Kind Bear* is her first children's book.